I0839846

THE PSYCHOLOGY OF CHARACTERS : THE ULTIMATE GUIDE TO CREATING YOUR HEROES AND ANTAGONISTS

AURNY AIRDUVAL

THE PSYCHOLOGY OF CHARACTERS : THE ULTIMATE GUIDE TO CREATING YOUR HEROES AND ANTAGONISTS

Foreword

You hold in your hands a genuine guide to explore the complex and captivating world of character psychology. You are about to uncover the depths of the human soul. You will learn how to create characters that will leave a lasting impression.

When we open a book, we enter a universe where characters become our friends, enemies, confidants, and mirrors. They are the vehicles through which we explore imaginary worlds and the human condition itself. From brave heroes to intriguing antagonists, passionate lovers to loyal friends, each character we encounter adds a unique dimension to the story.

This guide is designed to help you create characters who captivate, move, and inspire your readers. We will delve into secret motivations, unspoken desires, and hidden traumas that shape the psychology of each character. We will explore how internal conflicts, moral dilemmas, and complex relationships enrich your narratives and make your characters more human than ever.

Whether you are a beginner writer looking to enhance your skills or an experienced author eager to add depth to your characters, this guide is your travel companion. Each chapter will provide you with practical advice, concrete examples, and stimulating exercises to develop your characterization skills.

With our guide, prepare to explore the darkest and brightest corners of the human soul, bring unforgettable heroes and memorable antagonists to life, and write stories that touch the hearts of your readers.

Part 1

Introduction to character psychology

Chapter 1

The significance of character psychology

When we open a book, watch a film, or dive into a television series, we are drawn to the characters. They are the ones who captivate us, make us laugh, cry, gasp in surprise, or shock. Characters are at the heart of every story, and their psychology is the element that breathes life into these stories.

Character psychology is the key to creating engaging and memorable stories. Well-developed characters are the vehicles through which readers emotionally engage with the narrative. They drive the plot, create identification and empathy, serve as sources of complexity and conflict, and are the elements that make a story unforgettable.

We will explore why character psychology is of crucial importance in narrative writing. We will delve into the reasons why well-developed and psychologically rich characters are not only memorable but also essential for captivating your readers and making them emotionally attached to your story.

1. Characters are the engines of the story

Imagine a story without characters. It would be empty, devoid of emotion, and ultimately meaningless. Characters are the engines that propel the plot forward. Their actions, choices, and motivations bring the story to life. It is the characters who create conflict, make crucial decisions, and evolve throughout the narrative.

When readers emotionally invest in the characters, they automatically become invested in the story. They want to know what will happen to these characters, how they will overcome obstacles, and how they will evolve over time. Ultimately, it is the characters that make the story memorable.

2. Characters foster identification and empathy

For a reader to fully immerse themselves in a story, they must be able to identify with the characters. Readers seek characters with whom they can establish an emotional connection. This means they need to understand the motivations, fears, desires, and dilemmas of the characters.

When readers identify with a character, they feel what the character feels. They share in its joys and sorrows, and they experience the story through its eyes. This creates a powerful bond between the reader and the character, making them more inclined to continue reading and emotionally invest in the story.

3. The psychology of characters adds complexity

Well-developed characters are rarely one-dimensional. They have layers, contradictions, and internal conflicts. Their motivations can be ambivalent, their choices morally nuanced, and their emotions deep and ever-changing. This complexity makes characters more realistic and captivating.

When readers encounter complex characters, they are prompted to think more deeply about the themes and dilemmas explored in the story. They wonder why the characters do what they do, and this invites them to reflect on the nuances of human nature.

4. The psychology of characters creates interesting conflicts

Conflicts lie at the heart of any good story. Well-developed characters bring internal and external conflicts that fuel the plot. Their desires, fears, and motivations can lead to fascinating dilemmas and unexpected twists.

Readers are drawn to conflicts because they create tension and suspense. They want to see how characters will overcome obstacles and how their choices will lead to satisfying or tragic conclusions.

Chapter 2

Book objectives

Now that we have explored the significance of character psychology, it's time to clarify the objectives of this book. Why have you chosen to delve into character psychology, and what can you expect from this exploration?

1. Understanding the foundations of character psychology

One of the main objectives of this book is to provide you with a solid foundation in character psychology. You will discover the essential elements that make up a character's psychology, including motivations, traumas, hidden desires, and relational dynamics. Understanding these foundations is crucial for creating credible and engaging characters.

2. Creating memorable characters

Another key objective is to guide you in creating memorable characters. You will learn to avoid the pitfalls of stereotypical characters and develop protagonists and antagonists that will leave a lasting impression on your readers. We will explore techniques to make your characters unique, authentic, and unforgettable.

3. Using character psychology to strengthen your narrative

Character psychology is not just an academic exercise; it is a powerful tool to enhance your narrative. You will learn how to use character psychology to create interesting conflicts, captivating moments of transformation, and emotionally rich scenes. We will discuss specific techniques for integrating character psychology into the writing of your story.

4. Avoiding common mistakes in character creation

Creating compelling characters can be a challenge, and it's easy to fall into common pitfalls. One of our objectives is to help you avoid these mistakes. You will learn to identify flat, inconsistent, or stereotypical characters and how to correct them to align with your vision of the story.

5. Deepen your understanding through case studies

To help you visualize theory in action, we will examine case studies of famous characters from literature and cinema. You will see how talented writers have used character psychology to create literary icons.

These practical examples will inspire you in your own writing endeavors.

6. Becoming a accomplished character writer

The ultimate goal of this book is to help you become an accomplished character writer. We will provide you with the knowledge, skills, and tools necessary to create heroes and antagonists that will captivate your readers and breathe life into your stories. You will be able to master the art of character psychology and apply it with confidence in your writing projects. You will be ready to create characters that will linger in the memories of your readers long after they've closed your book.

Chapter 3

The impact of characters on the story and readers

Characters are much more than mere actors in a story. Characters are the central elements of any narrative. They drive the plot, carry themes, serve as sources of identification and emotion, create tension and conflict, and represent the most lasting memories for readers. They are the elements that bring your story to life and transform it into an immersive experience for your audience. Understanding how characters influence the story and the reader's experience is crucial for writers aiming to create unforgettable narratives. That's why we will delve into detail on how characters influence the story you tell and the experience your readers undergo.

1. Characters as drivers of the plot

Characters are the drivers of the plot. Their actions, decisions, and choices shape the unfolding of the story. Imagine a detective novel without the main detective solving the mystery, or an adventure narrative without the hero or heroine facing challenges. Characters are at the heart of the action, and it is their involvement in the plot that keeps readers captivated.

2. Characters as bearers of themes and messages

Characters also serve as vehicles for the themes and messages of your story. Their experiences, moral dilemmas, transformations, and internal conflicts can convey profound ideas to the readers. For example, a character on a quest for redemption can explore the theme of redemption, while a character faced with morally complex choices can provoke reflections on the nature of morality.

3. Characters as sources of identification and emotion

Identification is a key element for readers to emotionally invest in a story. Well-developed characters provide readers with points of identification, as these readers can see themselves through the characters. They share in their emotions, fears, and hopes. This emotional connection enhances the reading experience and makes the story more memorable.

4. Characters as sources of tension and conflict

Conflict is essential to maintain the interest of readers. Characters are often at the root of this conflict, whether through internal conflicts arising from their motivations and dilemmas, or external conflicts with other characters or external forces. Readers want to see how characters will resolve these conflicts, creating tension and suspense.

5. Characters as lasting memories

When well-written characters have a significant impact on the story and readers, they leave a lasting imprint. Readers remember characters who moved them, made them reflect, or captivated them. These characters become literary icons and continue to live in the minds of readers long after the book has been closed.

Part 2

The foundations of character psychology

Chapter 4

Character psychology explained

Character psychology is a crucial element in creating credible and captivating characters. It encompasses the motivations, emotions, beliefs, desires, and internal conflicts of your characters. Understanding these elements will enable you to develop rich and nuanced characters that breathe life into your story. But what does character psychology really mean, and how can you use it to enrich your heroes and antagonists? We will explore the foundations of character psychology to give you a solid understanding of this concept.

1. Character psychology in a word

Fundamentally, character psychology boils down to understanding how characters think, feel, and act. This includes their motivations, emotions, beliefs, desires, and fears. Character psychology encompasses the entirety of your characters' inner world, which, though fictional, must appear authentic to readers.

2. Motivation as the foundation of psychology

Motivation is one of the fundamental pillars of character psychology. Why do your characters do what they do? What drives them to act in certain ways? Motivations can be external (such as achieving a goal) or internal (like overcoming a deep-seated fear). Understanding your characters' motivations is essential to make their actions believable and coherent.

3. Emotions and emotional reactions

Emotions lie at the core of character psychology. Characters react to events in the story based on their emotions. For example, a character might react with anger to a betrayal, while another might react with sadness. How your characters handle their emotions shapes their development and influences their decisions.

4. Beliefs, values, and internal conflicts

The beliefs and values of characters are important elements of their psychology. These elements determine what they believe in, what they consider right or wrong, and what they are willing to fight for. Internal conflicts arise when characters face moral dilemmas due to their beliefs and values.

5. Desires and objectives

The desires and objectives of characters are closely tied to their psychology. Hidden desires, unspoken dreams, and personal goals add depth to your characters. The pursuit of these desires can create powerful motivations and fascinating conflicts.

6. Complexity and consistency

To create psychologically convincing characters, complexity and consistency are essential. Characters are not static; they evolve and change in response to events in the story. However, these changes must be consistent with the established psychology of the character. Complexity lies in how the different facets of a character's psychology intersect.

Chapter 5

The art of characterization

Characterization is the art of bringing your characters to life by imbuing them with distinctive and memorable traits through their appearance, behavior, speech, thoughts, and relationships. It is a crucial aspect of character psychology, as it allows readers to understand who your characters are and how they behave. We will delve into the techniques and strategies to create vivid and authentic characters.

1. Physical characterization

Physical characterization involves describing the physical appearance of your characters. This includes details such as height, hair color, dress style, facial features, and anything visible to the naked eye. Physical characterization can be used to give an initial impression of your characters, but it shouldn't stop there. It should be subtly integrated throughout the story to reinforce the reader's vision of the character.

2. Behavioral characterization

Behavioral characterization involves the actions, reactions, and behaviors of your characters. How do they behave in different situations? How do they react under pressure? Their behaviors reveal a lot about their personality and motivations. For example, a character who consistently reacts with anger to criticism may have a fragile ego.

3. Characterization through speech

The language and speech of your characters are powerful tools for characterization. Dialogues can reveal elements such as the level of education, tone of voice, sense of humor, familiar or sophisticated language, and even regional accents. The words your characters choose and how they use them speak volumes about their personality.

4. Characterization through thoughts and emotions

The inner thoughts and emotions of your characters are essential for creating deep characterization. Readers want to know what your characters feel and think. Inner monologues, personal reflections, and moments of vulnerability allow readers to dive into the minds of your characters and understand their secret motivations.

5. Characterization through interpersonal relationships

The relationships your characters have with other characters are another means of characterization. How do your characters treat their friends, family, enemies? Their interactions with others reveal aspects of their personality, such as loyalty, empathy, distrust, or their ability to manipulate.

6. Evolutionary characterization

Characters should not remain static throughout the story. They should evolve and change in response to events and challenges they face. This evolution should be consistent with their initial characterization. For example, a shy character may gain confidence over the course of the story, but this transformation must be well-constructed to be believable.

7. Characterization exercises

To refine your characterization skills, consider creating detailed character sheets. Write scenes or dialogues that highlight the features of your characters. You can also try writing inner monologues to explore the psychology of your characters in depth.

Chapter 6

Avoiding the pitfalls of stereotypical characters

When creating characters, it's tempting to fall into the trap of stereotypes, using predictable archetypes and clichéd traits. Avoiding the pitfalls of stereotypical characters is essential for crafting memorable and authentic characters. Stereotypes can make your story predictable, flat, and less engaging for readers. By developing well-rounded characters, subverting expectations, and creating complex motivations, you can bring to life unique characters that will captivate your readers. Let's now explore how to avoid the pitfalls of stereotypical characters and create unique and authentic personas.

1. Understanding stereotypes

Stereotypes are preconceived and simplified ideas about a group of people or a type of character. For example, the notion that a wizard is always wise and bearded, or that a private detective is always cynical and solitary. Using stereotypes can make your characters predictable and uninteresting.

2. Creating well-rounded characters

To avoid stereotypes, it's crucial to create well-rounded characters. This means they should have multiple and nuanced facets. For example, a character who appears tough may also have moments of vulnerability and tenderness. Complex characters are more believable and captivating.

3. Avoiding cliched traits

Cliched traits are personality traits or physical characteristics that are excessively used in literature or media. For example, the villain with a scar on the face or the eccentric university professor wearing round glasses. Avoid resorting to these cliches as they make your characters predictable.

4. Subverting expectations

An excellent way to avoid stereotypes is to subvert the reader's expectations. This means you can introduce a character who initially appears to fit a stereotype and then subvert it by giving them unexpected characteristics. For example, a strong and muscular man who is, in reality, a poetry enthusiast.

5. Giving complex motivations

The motivations of your characters are an excellent way to make them unique. Instead of giving a character a simple and obvious motivation, delve deeper. Ask yourself why they want what they want and how it fits into their psychology.

6. Drawing inspiration from reality

One of the best ways to create authentic characters is to draw inspiration from the real world. Observe people around you, study their behaviours, motivations, and complexities. Use these observations to enrich your characters.

7.Exercises to avoid stereotypes

To practice creating non-stereotypical characters, try taking a common stereotype and transforming it into something unexpected. For instance, take the archetype of the 'friendly neighbour' and imagine them as a secret international spy. Play with reader expectations to craft unique characters.

Part 3

Deep motivations

Chapter 7

External motivations and internal motivations

The motivations of your characters drive their behaviour and actions in the story. They can be divided into two main categories: external motivations and internal motivations. Understanding the difference between these two types of motivations is crucial for developing complex, believable, and captivating characters. External motivations are visible and measurable, while internal motivations are deeply rooted in the characters' psychology. By using these two types of motivations thoughtfully, you can bring characters to life with whom readers identify and emotionally invest.

1. External motivations

External motivations are goals, rewards, or external circumstances that drive a character to act. These motivations are often visible and measurable. For example, a character may be motivated by the search for treasure, the pursuit of a promotion, or the resolution of a mystery.

2. Internal motivations

Internal motivations are deeply rooted in a character's psychology. They are linked to their emotions, hidden desires, values, beliefs, and personal development. Internal motivations are often more complex and nuanced than external motivations.

3. Examples of external motivations

- The pursuit of a material reward, such as money, a precious object, or fame.
- Achieving a specific goal, such as winning a tournament, obtaining a degree, or solving a mystery.
- Survival in dangerous circumstances, such as escaping a predator or surviving a shipwreck.
- Conquering territory or seeking political power.

4. Examples of internal motivations

- The quest for identity or the search for meaning in life.
- Redemption for regrettable past actions.
- Struggling with inner demons, such as fear, anger, or guilt.
- Pursuing love, acceptance, or self-esteem.

5. Using both types of motivations

The most compelling characters are often those motivated by a combination of internal and external motivations. For example, a detective may be motivated by the desire to solve a murder (external motivation) while grappling with their own inner demons related to a past failure (internal motivation).

6. Conflicts and dilemmas

External and internal motivations can sometimes come into conflict or create dilemmas for your characters. For example, a character may face the decision to pursue a lucrative career (external motivation) at the expense of their artistic dreams (internal motivation). These conflicts add depth to your characters and fuel the plot.

7. Evolution of motivations

Your characters' motivations should not remain static. They can evolve throughout the story in response to events, interactions, and internal reflections of the characters. This evolution makes the characters more credible and human.

Chapter 8

Understanding characters' desires and goals

Understanding the desires and goals of your characters is essential for developing rich and believable psychology. The desires and goals of your characters are fundamental elements of their psychology. They form the basis of their motivations and actions in the story. Hidden desires, concrete goals, goal conflicts, and changes in desires can all contribute to making your characters captivating and complex. By skillfully using these elements in your narrative, you can create unforgettable characters and evoke strong empathy from your readers. We will explore in detail how to understand, develop, and use the desires and goals of your characters to enrich your narrative.

1. Hidden desires

Hidden desires are the dreams, hopes, and deep wishes of your characters. They may be buried beneath the surface and not immediately apparent to other characters or readers. For example, a character may desire to reconcile with a parent they haven't seen in years.

2. Concrete goals

Concrete goals are specific and measurable objectives that your characters actively pursue in the story. These can include professional, personal, romantic, or even heroic quests. For instance, a character may have the goal of becoming the best detective in the city.

3. Short-term goals and long-term goals

The goals of your characters can vary in terms of duration. Some may be short-term, such as passing an exam, while others may be long-term, like saving the world. The combination of these two types of goals can create an interesting dynamic in the story.

4. Goal Conflicts

Goal conflicts occur when the desires or goals of two characters collide. These conflicts can create tension and suspense in the plot. For example, two characters may be competing for the same job.

5. Desires that evolve

The desires and goals of your characters should not remain static. They can evolve throughout the story in response to events, interactions, and internal reflections. For example, a character may initially seek revenge, but as the story progresses, they may realize that reconciliation is a better path.

6. Desires that drive transformations

Deep-seated desires can be the catalyst for significant transformations in your characters. When a character actively pursues a desire or goal, it can propel them to overcome obstacles, grow as an individual, or change their perspective on life.

7. Using desires to forge emotional connections

The desires and goals of your characters are an excellent means of creating emotional connections with readers. Readers can identify with the characters' desires and struggles, making them more invested in the story. The emotions evoked by the characters' desires and goals can render your narrative more potent and memorable.

Chapter 9

Examples of powerful motivations

The motivations of your characters are a key element in bringing their actions and decisions to life. Powerful motivations are an essential component for adding depth to your characters and your story. They make your characters more believable and captivating for readers. Whether it's the quest for truth, vengeance, survival, or love, motivations can propel your characters into thrilling adventures and create emotional connections with readers. By skillfully using them, you can enrich the psychology of your characters and make your narrative more engaging. Let's explore several examples of powerful motivations that you can use to enhance your characters.

1.The quest for truth

The quest for truth is a powerful motivation that can lead a character to explore mysteries, uncover hidden secrets, or unravel lies surrounding their past. For instance, a character may be obsessed with searching for the truth behind the mysterious disappearance of their father.

2. Revenge

Revenge is an emotionally charged motivation that can drive a character to pursue those who have wronged them and seek to mete out punishment. This motivation can create moral conflicts and intriguing dilemmas. For instance, a character may seek revenge for the death of their best friend.

3. Survival

Survival is a fundamental motivation that drives characters to struggle against obstacles and dangers to stay alive. This motivation is often utilized in survival contexts, such as a deserted island or a post-apocalyptic world.

4. Love

Love is a powerful motivation that can take many forms, from romantic love to familial love or deep friendship. Characters can be motivated to do anything to protect or reunite with a loved one. For example, a character might embark on a perilous journey to save their kidnapped child.

5. Personal Fulfillment

Personal fulfillment is a motivation that drives characters to reach their full potential, fulfill their dreams, or overcome their limitations. This can include professional, artistic, or athletic goals. For example, a character may aspire to become a world-renowned musician.

6. Justice

The pursuit of justice is a motivation that drives characters to fight for what they consider fair and equitable. They may seek to triumph over injustice in a corrupt system or reveal the truth about an unjust case. For example, a character may become a lawyer to defend the wrongly accused.

7. Redemption

Redemption is a profound motivation that drives characters to seek forgiveness for their past mistakes. They may be haunted by guilt and seek to make amends for the wrongs they have caused. For example, a former criminal may dedicate themselves to helping others to redeem their past actions.

8. Exploration

Exploration is a motivation that drives characters to discover new horizons, push the limits of their knowledge, or venture into the unknown. This can include journeys to distant lands, the search for lost treasures, or the exploration of fantastical worlds.

9. Freedom

The pursuit of freedom is a powerful motivation that can drive characters to escape captivity, break the chains of oppression, or fight for their rights. For example, a character may be a slave seeking freedom.

10. Using motivations subtly

When incorporating these motivations into your story, ensure to develop them subtly and integrate them cohesively into the psychology of your characters. Powerful motivations can create intricate narrative arcs and unforgettable characters.

Part 4

The past and traumas of characters

Chapter 10

The influence of the past on characters

The past of your characters is a key element of their psychology. The influence of the past on characters is essential for developing rich and credible psychology. Traumas, relationships, choices, and past events shape the personalities of your characters and influence their actions and decisions. They all have a profound impact on who your characters are and how they respond to present challenges. By exploring the past of your characters subtly and strategically, you can create complex and memorable characters that enhance your narrative. We will explore how the past influences your characters and how to use it to enrich your story.

1. The traumas of the past

The traumas of the past are traumatic events or painful experiences that your characters have lived through. These traumas can include losses, abuses, accidents, emotional injuries, or any other experience that has left scars. The traumas of the past can influence the fears, phobias, and self-destructive behaviors of your characters.

2. The relationships of the past

Past relationships, whether positive or negative, have an impact on how your characters interact with others. Family relationships, friendships, past loves, and sworn enemies can all shape the psychology of your characters. For example, a character may struggle to trust due to past betrayals.

3. Choices and regrets of the past

The choices and regrets of the past are elements that often haunt your characters. Decisions made in the past, whether good or bad, can have lasting consequences. Characters may be haunted by regrets and seek to rectify their past mistakes.

4. Determining events

Certain events from the past can be determining factors in the personality and psychology of your characters. For example, a character may have survived a plane crash that shaped their fear of flying, or a child who grew up in poverty may have developed a fierce ambition to escape that situation.

5. Flashbacks and revelations

Flashbacks and revelations about your characters' past can be powerful tools to explore their psychology. They allow readers to delve into the characters' past experiences and understand what truly motivates them.

Flashbacks can be used strategically to reveal key elements of the story.

6. The evolution of the past

Your characters' pasts should not remain static. It can evolve throughout the story based on new experiences and choices. For example, a character may start haunted by a past trauma, but over the course of the story, they may find healing and resilience.

7. Using the past to create conflicts and narrative arcs

Your characters' pasts can be used to create interesting internal and external conflicts. Revelations about the past can cause upheavals in the plot and emotional dilemmas for your characters. They can also be the source of powerful transformative narrative arcs.

Chapter 11

Trauma and character behavior

Traumas are devastating experiences that leave deep scars in the psychology of your characters. These traumas have a significant impact on their behavior, emotions, and relationships. They serve as powerful elements to influence the behavior and psychology of your characters. They can create complex and nuanced characters, but it is important to handle them with care and integrate them thoughtfully into your narrative. Reactions to trauma, defense mechanisms, phobias, and attempts at healing are all aspects to explore in order to create credible and emotionally rich characters. We will explore how traumas influence the behavior of your characters and how to use them to develop credible and nuanced characters.

1. Reactions to trauma

Reactions to trauma vary from individual to individual. Some characters may become anxious, withdrawn, or depressed, while others may become angry, impulsive, or obsessive. It is essential to choose the trauma reaction that aligns with your character's personality and the nature of the trauma.

2. Defense mechanisms

Traumatized characters often develop defense mechanisms to cope with their pain. This can include dissociation, denial, rationalization, or projection. These mechanisms can lead to unusual behaviors or unexpected emotional responses.

3. Flashbacks and nightmares

Flashbacks and nightmares are common manifestations of trauma in your characters' lives. They may mentally relive the traumatic event, which can lead them to experience the intense emotion associated with the trauma.

4. Phobias and avoidance

Traumatized characters may develop phobias related to the traumatic event or associated stimuli. They may also seek to avoid anything that reminds them of the trauma. These phobias and avoidance behaviors can create obstacles for your characters in the story.

5. Interpersonal relationships

Trauma can have a significant impact on the interpersonal relationships of your characters. They may struggle to trust, open up emotionally, or form intimate bonds. Trauma can also lead to conflicts with other characters.

6. Attempts at Healing and Recovery

Some traumatized characters may embark on a journey of healing and recovery to overcome their trauma. This may involve therapy, seeking social support, or pursuing personal redemption. These healing journeys can be powerful for your characters.

7. Using trauma to create narrative arcs

Trauma can be used to create compelling transformative narrative arcs. Your characters can evolve throughout the story by overcoming their traumas and finding healing. However, it's important to handle these themes with sensitivity and conduct research to represent them authentically.

<h1 style="text-align:center">Chapter 12</h1>

<h2 style="text-align:center">Integrating the past into the story</h2>

The past of your characters is a valuable resource to enrich your story and develop captivating characters. Skillfully integrating the past into your narrative can strengthen the psychology of your characters, create powerful narrative arcs, enhance the plot, and evoke empathy from readers. Use flashbacks, meaningful dialogues, parallels with the past, and gradually reveal details to create memorable characters and captivating stories. We will explore how to effectively integrate the past of your characters.

1. Using strategic flashbacks

Flashbacks are a powerful tool to explore the past of your characters. They allow you to vividly and immersively depict past events. Use strategic flashbacks to reveal key elements of your characters' past at the right moments in the story. Ensure that the flashbacks are relevant to the current plot and contribute to the understanding of the character.

2. Crafting meaningful dialogues

Dialogues between characters can be an opportunity to unveil details about their past. Confessions, revelations, and discussions about past events can help deepen relationships between characters and bring their personal stories to life.

3. Drawing parallels with the past

Establish parallels between the past events of your characters and the challenges they face in the present. This can reinforce the significance of current events and demonstrate how past experiences influence the decisions and actions of your characters.

4. Gradually unveil the past

Don't disclose all the details of your characters' past at once. Gradually reveal elements throughout the story to maintain the readers' interest. The mystery surrounding the past can be a source of suspense and intrigue.

5. Create emotional connections

Use the past to forge emotional connections between readers and your characters. Showcase the challenges they've overcome, the sacrifices they've made, and the moments of joy and pain they've experienced. Readers can identify with shared human experiences, making them more invested in the story.

6. Explore the consequences of the past

Past events have lasting consequences. Explore these consequences in your story. Show how past choices and events affect the characters in the present. The repercussions of the past can create interesting conflicts and dilemmas.

7. The returns from the past

Characters from the past can reappear in the story, creating unexpected returns. Reunions with old friends, enemies, or lost loves can add complexity to the plot and relationships.

8. The evolution of the past

Remember that the past of your characters can evolve throughout the story based on their new experiences and choices. This evolution can create rich and dynamic narrative arcs.

Part 5

Hidden desires and internal conflicts

Chapter 13

Revealing secret desires

The secret desires of your characters are a source of tension, intrigue, and character development. Unveiling these desires at the right moment in your story can create suspense, captivate readers, and deepen the psychology of your characters. Use dialogue, internal monologues, internal conflicts, and moments of revelation to bring these hidden desires to life. Secret desires can be a source of tension and intrigue in your story, while adding complexity to your characters. We will explore how to effectively reveal the secret desires of your characters.

1. Building suspense

Secret desires are often shrouded in mystery and suspense. Use this mystery to keep readers engaged and encourage them to learn more about your characters. Questions like "What is this character hiding?" or "What is their true desire?" can compel them to keep reading."

2. Using dialogues and inner monologues

Dialogues and inner monologues are powerful means of unveiling the secret desires of your characters. The inner thoughts of your characters can expose what they truly feel and deeply desire. Interactions between characters can also provide subtle hints about their secret desires.

3. Creating internal conflicts

Secret desires can generate internal conflicts for your characters. They may find themselves torn between their hidden desires and their apparent responsibilities or values. These internal conflicts can add complexity to their characters.

4. Gradually revealing secret desires

Don't unveil all your characters' secret desires at once. Disclose them gradually throughout the story to maintain suspense. Each revelation should have an impact on the plot and character development.

5. Creating moments of revelation

Craft powerful moments of revelation where the secret desires of your characters are finally unveiled. These moments can be turning points in the plot and emotional climaxes. Ensure that the revelation is significant and has an impact on the story.

6. Exploring the consequences of secret desires

Secret desires have consequences, whether for the character themselves or for others. Explore these consequences in your story. How do secret desires influence the actions and decisions of the characters? How do they affect relationships between characters?

7. Secret desires as the engine of the plot

Secret desires can also drive the plot. They can lead characters into quests, adventures, or conflicts as they seek to fulfill their hidden desires. Secret desires can be the source of unexpected twists in the plot.

Chapter 14

Using internal conflicts to create complex characters

Internal conflicts are an effective way to create complex and nuanced characters. They allow for the exploration of moral dilemmas, conflicts of loyalty, identity struggles, and many other aspects of your characters' psychology. They add depth to your characters' psychology, making them more realistic. By skillfully using internal conflicts, you can make your characters more engaging and your story richer. We will explore how to use internal conflicts to create unforgettable characters.

1. Defining internal conflicts

Internal conflicts occur when characters face tough choices, moral dilemmas, or inner conflicts. These conflicts can result from conflicting desires, values in conflict, or tumultuous pasts.

2. Creating ambivalent characters

Ambivalent characters are those who are neither entirely good nor entirely bad. They face tough choices, and their actions may vary depending on circumstances. Ambivalent characters are often more realistic and intriguing for readers.

3. Moral conflicts

Moral conflicts are ethical dilemmas that characters face. For example, a character may have to choose between revealing the truth at the expense of someone they love or protecting that person by remaining silent. Moral conflicts can provoke reflection in readers and make your characters more human.

4. Loyalty conflicts

Loyalty conflicts occur when characters must choose between two seemingly incompatible loyalties. For example, a character may be torn between loyalty to their family and loyalty to their duty to society. These conflicts add complexity to the psychology of your characters.

5. Identity conflicts

Identity conflicts occur when characters question their own identity, beliefs, or values. These conflicts can be profound and transform the way a character sees themselves and interacts with the world around them.

6. Internal conflicts as an engine of the plot

Internal conflicts can be the engine of the plot. The tough decisions made by characters due to these conflicts can lead to plot twists, unexpected consequences, and captivating plot developments.

7. The evolution of internal conflicts

Internal conflicts should not remain static. They can evolve throughout the story as characters learn, grow, and change. Evolving internal conflicts can be the catalyst for powerful narrative arcs of transformation.

Chapter 15

Moral and emotional dilemmas

Moral and emotional dilemmas are powerful tools to enrich the psychology of your characters and create captivating situations in your story. Dilemmas can have a significant impact on their psychology. They can highlight the values, emotions, and convictions of your characters while providing opportunities for character development. Skillful use of these dilemmas can make your narrative more engaging and your characters more memorable. Let's explore how to use moral and emotional dilemmas to enrich your characters and your story.

1. Moral dilemmas

Moral dilemmas are situations in which characters face difficult choices involving ethical questions. For example, a character may have to choose between saving the life of an innocent person at the expense of their own safety or leaving that person in danger to protect themselves.

2. Emotional dilemmas

Emotional dilemmas involve the emotions and relationships of the characters. For example, a character may be torn between the love they feel for two people and have to choose with whom they want to be. These emotional dilemmas can create intense internal conflicts.

3. Loyalty dilemmas

Loyalty dilemmas occur when characters must choose between their loyalty to different people, groups, or causes. For example, a character may be loyal to their childhood friend but must choose between supporting their friend or advocating for a just cause.

4. Survival dilemmas

Survival dilemmas occur when characters are faced with situations where their own survival is at stake. They may have to make desperate decisions to escape deadly dangers.

5. Dilemmas as character tests

Moral and emotional dilemmas can serve as character tests for your characters. They reveal the true nature of your characters by showing how they react to difficult choices. This can strengthen the psychology of your characters and contribute to their development.

6. The consequences of dilemmas

The choices your characters make during dilemmas have consequences that can impact the plot and relationships between characters. The consequences of dilemmas can create fascinating narrative arcs.

7. Creating realistic dilemmas

When creating dilemmas for your characters, ensure they are realistic and consistent with the psychology of your characters. Dilemmas should be complex enough to provoke thought but also credible enough for readers to identify with the characters.

Part 6

Interpersonal relationships

Chapter 16

Interactions between characters

Interactions between characters are a crucial element of character psychology and plot development. They shape relationships, group dynamics, and character psychology. Create dynamic relationships, meaningful conflicts, and revealing dialogues to bring your characters to life and engage readers. Interactions between characters can be a source of tension, character development, and intrigue in your story. We will explore how to create interactions between your characters that enrich your narrative and develop their psychology.

1. The dynamics of relationships

Each relationship between characters is unique and brings its own dynamics to the story. Close friends will have a different dynamic than rivals or lovers. Understand the nature of each relationship to create authentic interactions.

2. Conflicts and tensions

Conflicts and tensions between characters are sources of dramatic conflict. They can arise from disagreements, rivalries, secrets, or fundamental differences. These conflicts add depth to the characters and the plot.

3. Nonverbal communication

Nonverbal communication, such as facial expressions, body language, and gestures, is a crucial element of interactions between characters. Use it to convey unspoken emotions and subtleties in dialogues.

4. Meaningful dialogues

Dialogues between characters provide an opportunity to showcase their thoughts, emotions, and motivations. Create meaningful dialogues that reveal the psychology of your characters and advance the plot.

5. Evolution of relationships

The relationships between characters should not remain static. They can evolve throughout the story based on events and choices made by the characters. Characters may grow closer, drift apart, or even change allegiances.

6. Alliances and betrayals

Alliances and betrayals are key elements of character interactions. Characters may form alliances to achieve common goals, but these alliances can also be tested. Betrayals can create unexpected twists in the story.

7. Romantic and friendly relationships

Romantic and friendly relationships are powerful elements for developing the psychology of your characters. Explore the complexities of romantic relationships, deep friendships, and unwavering loyalties.

8. The consequences of interactions

Interactions between characters have repercussions that impact the plot and character development. Decisions made during interactions can have long-term consequences.

9. Character growth through interactions

Interactions between characters can be opportunities for growth and development for your characters. They can learn from each other, overcome conflicts, and evolve as individuals.

10. Consistency in interactions

Ensure that interactions between characters are consistent with their psychology and characterization. Characters should react authentically to situations and other characters.

Chapter 17

Creating authentic relationships

Character relationships are a key element of any story, and for them to be memorable and engaging, they must be authentic. Creating authentic relationships among your characters is essential to enrich your story and bring your characters to life. Understand their motivations, avoid stereotypes, create common ground and realistic conflicts, and show the evolution of relationships throughout the story. Authentic relationships will make your narrative more captivating, and your characters more memorable. We'll explore how to create authentic relationships among your characters, making them credible and emotionally rich.

1. Understand the motivations and pasts of characters

To create authentic relationships, it is essential to understand the motivations, pasts, and hidden desires of each character. This will help you determine how they interact with each other and how their relationships evolve.

2. Avoid clichés and stereotypes

Stereotypical and clichéd relationships can make your characters and your story predictable and uninteresting. Avoid the pitfalls of relationships like the 'loyal friend,' 'arch-enemy,' or 'perfect love.' Seek to subvert expectations and create unique dynamics.

3. Create common ground and realistic conflicts

Authentic relationships are built on common ground and realistic conflicts. Explore shared interests, common values, but also differences that can lead to disagreements and tensions. Common ground can strengthen bonds, while conflicts can add complexity.

4. Use communication and miscommunication

Communication is at the heart of relationships, but miscommunication can also play a crucial role in the plot. Misunderstandings, secrets, and unspoken words can create moments of tension and emotion.

5. Show the evolution of relationships

Character relationships are not static. They evolve throughout the story based on events, choices, and experiences. Show how characters grow together or drift apart.

6. Create moments of emotional connection

Moments of emotional connection are key in character relationships. They can be moments of vulnerability, mutual support, or revelation of deep truths. These moments strengthen the bonds between characters.

7. Avoid fixating on romantic relationships

While romantic relationships are important, don't solely focus your attention on them. Friendships, family relationships, and professional connections are equally crucial for the psychology of your characters.

8. Be consistent with character psychology

Ensure that interactions between characters are consistent with their psychology and characterization. Characters should react authentically to others and to situations.

9. Leave room for evolution and surprise

Don't be afraid to let your relationships surprise the readers. Characters can evolve unexpectedly, alliances can form and break, and relationships can take unexpected turns.

Chapter 18

Conflicts, alliances, and relationship developments

The relationships between characters are never static. They evolve throughout the story in response to conflicts, alliances, and the choices characters make. These elements are key factors in developing interactions between your characters convincingly. They add complexity to your characters and the plot, reflecting the ever-changing psychology of your characters. By skillfully using these elements, you can make your characters and your story richer and more engaging. We will explore how to use these elements to develop relationships between your characters convincingly.

1. Conflicts as the engine of the plot

Conflicts between characters can be a source of tension and intrigue. They can be caused by disagreements, rivalries, misunderstandings, or conflicting goals. Conflicts add depth to relationships and create opportunities for character development.

2. Strategic alliances

Characters can form strategic alliances to achieve common goals or to face external threats. These alliances can create interesting dynamics and plot twists.

3. Fragile alliances

Not all alliances are strong. Some are fragile and can be tested by internal conflicts, secrets, or betrayals. Fragile alliances add tension to the plot.

4. Developments in romantic relationships

Romantic relationships can evolve throughout the story. Characters may grow closer, drift apart, reconcile, or part ways. These developments reflect the growth and change of the characters.

5. The repercussions of conflicts and alliances

Conflicts and alliances have repercussions that impact the plot and characters. The decisions made during these interactions can have long-term consequences on relationships.

6. Moments of revelation

Moments of revelation are key moments where truths are unveiled, secrets are revealed, or hidden motivations come to light. These moments can transform relationships and the plot.

7. The impact of characters' choices

The impact of characters' choices in conflicts and alliances is crucial. These choices reveal their character, priorities, and values. The consequences of these choices can be lasting.

8. The complexity of family relationships

Family relationships are often complex and rich in emotions. Explore conflicts, loyalties, rivalries, and reconciliations within your characters' families.

9. The role of third parties in relationships

Third parties, whether other characters or external events, can influence the relationships between characters. They can act as catalysts for conflicts or factors that bring characters closer.

Part 7

The transformation of characters

Chapter 19

The character arc

The character arc is the journey of transformation that your characters undergo throughout the story. It is a crucial element for adding depth to the psychology of your characters and for developing that psychology. Create meaningful character arcs by guiding your characters through choices, conflicts, and transformations. Character arcs will make your characters more captivating and your story more engaging. We will explore how to create significant character arcs for your characters.

1. Understanding the character arc

The character arc is the process through which a character evolves, changes, and develops throughout the story. It can involve a positive, negative, or ambiguous transformation, depending on the character's choices and experiences.

2. The beginning of the character arc

The character arc begins with the introduction of the character and the establishment of their initial situation. Readers should understand who the character is at the beginning of the story and what their motivations and weaknesses are.

3. Conflict and growth

Conflict is often the catalyst for the character arc. Characters face challenges, obstacles, and dilemmas that compel them to question their beliefs, overcome their weaknesses, and evolve

4. The stages of the character arc

The character arc can be divided into key stages, including awareness, resistance to change, transformation, crisis, and resolution. Each of these stages contributes to the character's psychology.

5. Determining choices

The choices the character makes are at the heart of their character arc. These choices can be influenced by their motivations, values, and relationships with other characters. The consequences of these choices shape the character's psychology.

6. The consequences of the character arc

The character arc has consequences that affect the character themselves, other characters, and the plot.

The character's transformations can create twists, revelations, and moments of emotional clarity.

7. The conclusion of the character arc

The character arc typically concludes with a resolution that shows how the character has changed and what they have learned. This conclusion can be satisfying, emotional, or ambiguous, depending on the story.

8. Secondary character arcs

Don't forget about the character arcs of secondary characters. They contribute to the overall story by bringing unique perspectives and influencing the development of the main characters.

9. The consistency of the character arc

Ensure that the character arc is consistent with the character's psychology and the plot. The character's changes should be motivated and believable.

Chapter 20

Crucial decision moments

Crucial decision moments are pivotal instances in the story where characters face decisive choices that will have a significant impact on their psychology and the plot. They are powerful tools for developing the psychology of your characters and creating an emotionally rich plot. Create decisive choices that reveal the character of your characters, influence the plot, and captivate readers. We will now explore how to create these moments to make your characters more complex and your story more captivating.

1. Choices that reveal character

Crucial decision moments are an opportunity to reveal the true nature of your characters. The choices they make in these moments **showcase their motivations, values, and priorities.**

2. Moral and ethical dilemmas

Moral and ethical dilemmas are particularly powerful moments of crucial decision. Characters are faced with choices where there is no easy answer, and their decisions reveal their moral integrity.

3. Choices that impact the plot

Crucial decision moments can also have a significant impact on the plot. The characters' choices can change the course of the story, trigger plot twists, or influence the actions of other characters.

4. Internal conflicts

Crucial decision moments often reflect internal conflicts within characters. They may be torn between conflicting desires, conflicting loyalties, or deep moral dilemmas.

5. The repercussions of choices

The choices made in crucial decision moments have consequences that affect the rest of the story. These repercussions can create narrative tension and opportunities for character development.

6. Resolution moments

Some crucial decision moments are resolution moments where characters overcome obstacles, make significant decisions, and head towards the conclusion of their character arc.

7. Moments of emotional clarity

Crucial decision moments can also be moments of emotional clarity where characters finally understand their own motivations and emotions. These revelatory moments can be emotionally powerful.

8. Unexpected choices

Don't be afraid to surprise readers by having your characters make unexpected choices. These choices can add complexity and authenticity to your characters.

9. The importance of preparation

For crucial decision moments to have emotional impact, it is essential to prepare the ground by developing the psychology of your characters and building the stakes of the plot.

Chapter 21

Avoid abrupt character changes

When developing the psychology of your characters and their character arcs, it's important to avoid abrupt and inconsistent character changes. Maintaining the credibility of your characters and your story is crucial. Ensure that character developments are consistent, gradual, and motivated by the psychology of the characters. Well-executed character changes make characters more memorable and the plot more engaging. We'll explore how to maintain consistency in the evolution of your characters to make it credible and captivating.

1. Psychological consistency

Psychological consistency is crucial for character changes to be believable. Characters must evolve in a manner consistent with their established psychology, motivations, and past experiences.

2. Setting the stage

For character changes to be convincing, it is necessary to set the stage by revealing the motivations and hidden desires of the characters. Readers must understand why a character makes a particular choice.

3. The gradual stages of evolution

Character changes should occur gradually, in stages. Characters should not go from one extreme to the other overnight. Small, progressive transformations are more realistic.

4. Moments of reflection

Moments of reflection are opportunities for characters to question their beliefs, make important choices, and become aware of their evolution. These moments add depth to the character arc.

5. Internal conflicts

Character changes often result from internal conflicts. Characters may be torn between conflicting desires, values in conflict, or shared loyalties.

6. The consequences of choices

Show the consequences of characters' choices on their development. Choices can have positive or negative repercussions, enhancing the credibility of character changes.

7. Avoid narrative shortcuts

Avoid narrative shortcuts such as a sudden personality change to resolve a plot issue. Readers are more invested in the story when character changes are well-developed.

8. The complexity of characters

Complex characters undergo nuanced changes in character. They may be in conflict with themselves, make difficult choices, and experience moments of vulnerability.

9. Perseverance and backtracking

Characters may make mistakes along the way and regress in their development. This adds depth to their character arcs and reflects the reality of personal growth.

Part 8

Practical tools

Chapter 22

Exercises to understand your characters

A deep understanding of your characters is essential for creating compelling psychology. We'll explore practical exercises to help you better understand your characters, their motivations, and their evolution throughout the story. This will allow you to delve into their psychology and create more easily memorable and authentic characters. A profound knowledge of your characters' psychology will enrich your story and make readers more invested in their journeys.

1. Character interview

Imagine that you are conducting an interview with your character. Ask them questions about their past, dreams, fears, desires, and motivations. Write down your character's responses to better understand their psychology.

2. Character's diary

Create a diary for your character. Encourage them to write down their most intimate thoughts, reflections on the events of the story, and emotions. This diary can provide you with a profound insight into your character's psychology.

3. Vision board

Create a vision board for your character using images, words, and symbols that represent their goals, aspirations, and psychology. This can help you visually visualize the complexity of your character.

4. The character's letters

Write letters that your character might send to other characters in the story, even if they are never actually sent. These letters can reveal the character's unspoken thoughts and emotions.

5. Flashback scenes

Write flashback scenes that explore your character's past. These scenes can show key moments in their life that have influenced their psychology and development.

6. Internal monologue

Write an internal monologue for your character during a crucial moment in the story. This will allow you to delve deep into their thoughts, doubts, and motivations.

7. The motivation test

Ask yourself: 'Why is your character acting this way?' List both internal and external motivations that drive them to make specific decisions. This will help you understand the forces that guide their behavior.

8. The 'what if' scenarios

Imagine different 'What If' scenarios for your character. For instance, 'What if your character had made a different choice at a key moment in the story?' Explore how these alternative scenarios would have affected their psychology and journey.

9. Beta reader feedback

Have your work read by beta readers and ask them to provide feedback on the psychology of your characters. External feedback can reveal aspects you may not have noticed.

10. Continuous revision

Understanding the psychology of your characters evolves throughout the writing process. Regularly review your characters as the story progresses to ensure their psychology remains consistent and convincing.

Chapter 23

Questionnaires and character sheets

Questionnaires and character sheets are practical tools for organizing and delving into the psychology of your characters. The use of questionnaires and character sheets is an effective way to explore the psychology of your characters and make them richer and more believable. These tools will help you organize important details of your characters' lives, from their motivations to their internal conflicts. A better understanding of your characters will enrich your narrative and captivate your readers more deeply. We will see how to use them to create richer and more complex characters.

1. Character questionnaires

Character questionnaires are lists of questions designed to explore various aspects of your characters' psychology. They can cover areas such as background, motivations, desires, fears, and relationships.

2. Character sheets

Character sheets are organized documents that list important details about each character. They typically include information about appearance, personality, relationships, goals, and internal conflicts of the character.

3. Fundamental questions

When creating character questionnaires, start with fundamental questions such as: "Who is this character?" "What are their motivations?" "What are their desires?" "What are their obstacles?" These questions will lay the groundwork for the character's psychology.

4. Context questions

Explore the context and backgrounds of your characters. Ask yourself: "What is this character's past?" "What is their education?" "What are their past experiences that have influenced their psychology?"

5. Motivation questions

Motivations are essential to understand why a character acts in certain ways. Ask questions about the character's short and long-term goals, what drives them to act, and what they seek to accomplish.

6. Relationship questions

Examine the character's relationships with other characters in the story. Who are their allies? Who are their adversaries? How do these relationships influence their psychology?

7. Internal conflict questions

Internal conflicts add complexity to the character's psychology. Ask yourself: "What are the internal struggles of this character?" "What are their moral dilemmas?" "What are their fears and doubts?"

8. Character change questions

If your character undergoes a transformation throughout the story, explore the stages of this change. Ask questions about the pivotal moments and choices that led to this evolution.

9. The use of character sheets

Character sheets are a visual way to organize information about your characters. Create a sheet for each main character and update these sheets as the story progresses.

10. Revision and deepening

Regularly revisit the character questionnaires and sheets to revise and deepen them as you develop the story. This ongoing revision will strengthen the consistency of your characters' psychology.

Chapter 24

Character Psychology in Scene Writing

The psychology of your characters is crucial to bring your scenes to life and make interactions between characters believable and engaging. It is a key element for writing captivating scenes. Integrate the motivations, emotions, internal conflicts, and goals of the characters into each scene to create authentic and engaging interactions. When you master the art of incorporating character psychology into your scenes, you breathe life into your characters and enhance the emotional impact of your story. Let's explore how to integrate character psychology into scene writing.

1. Character motivation

Every action and dialogue of the characters should stem from their internal motivations and goals. When writing a scene, ask yourself what each character seeks to achieve and how it influences their behavior.

2. Emotional reactions

Emotions play a crucial role in the psychology of characters. Express the emotions of your characters authentically by showing their emotional reactions to events and dialogues in the scene.

3. Internal And External Conflicts

Internal conflicts, such as moral dilemmas, and external conflicts, such as disagreements with other characters, can add tension to a scene. Explore how these conflicts influence the actions and words of your characters.

4. Scene objectives

Each scene should have a specific goal in the development of the story or characters. Ensure that the actions and dialogues of the characters contribute to achieving this goal.

5. Meaningful dialogues

Dialogues are a powerful means of revealing the psychology of characters. Use conversations to explore the thoughts, motivations, and relationships of your characters.

6. Internal monologues

Internal monologues allow readers to delve deep into a character's thoughts and emotions. Use them to reveal internal reflections and inner conflicts.

7. Gestures and facial expressions

Gestures and facial expressions are subtle ways to depict the psychology of characters. Describe these elements to bring emotional reactions and intentions of your characters to life.

8. Moments of revelation

Scenes can be an opportunity to unveil crucial elements of the characters' psychology, such as secrets, hidden desires, or past traumas. Use these moments to create emotional plot twists.

9. Conflicts and evolutions of relationships

Scenes can serve as breaking points or moments of closeness in character relationships. Explore how interactions in a scene influence the dynamics of relationships.

10. Consistency of character psychology

Ensure that character psychology remains consistent from one scene to another. Character changes should be motivated by the character's arc and events in the story.

Part 9

Avoiding common mistakes

Chapter 25

The pitfalls of character creation

Character creation is a complex task, and it's easy to fall into certain common traps. Avoiding these common pitfalls in character creation is essential to craft memorable and convincing characters. Take the time to develop the psychology of your characters, make them nuanced, and ensure they evolve coherently. Steer clear of clichés, stereotypes, and characterization mistakes to create unforgettable heroes and antagonists. We'll explore common mistakes to avoid in character creation to ensure they are memorable and compelling.

1. The stereotype

One of the most common pitfalls is creating stereotypical characters that fit into clichés. Avoid giving your characters superficial traits based on overly familiar archetypes.

2. Lack of complexity

Flat characters lack depth and authenticity. Avoid oversimplifying the psychology of your characters or making them one-dimensional.

3. Inconsistent psychology

Consistency is essential in character psychology. Avoid having your characters act in a way that is inconsistent with their established motivations or development.

4. Heavy exposition

Avoid revealing character psychology through heavy and explanatory exposition. Instead, show their psychology through their actions, dialogues, and reactions.

5. Characters too perfect

Characters that are too perfect lack challenges and interesting conflicts. Avoid creating characters without flaws or weaknesses, as it makes them less convincing.

6. Inconsistency in character arcs

Inconsistent character arcs can confuse readers. Ensure that character development is motivated and logical, avoiding sudden and unexplained changes.

7. Lack of clear motivation

Character motivations should be clear to readers. Avoid having your characters act without understandable motivations.

8. Lack of internal conflict

Internal conflict is a key element of character psychology. Avoid creating characters without moral dilemmas, hidden desires, or internal struggles.

9. The overly predictable reaction

Characters should not always react predictably to events. Avoid making your characters' reactions too conforming to expectations, as it can make the story less engaging.

10. Forgetting secondary characters

Don't overlook the development of secondary characters. Avoid making them insignificant or underdeveloped, as they can contribute to enriching the story.

11. Lack of growth

Characters should evolve throughout the story. Avoid creating static characters who do not change, as it can make the story less interesting.

12. Lack of research

If you're writing about characters with experiences or cultural contexts different from your own, avoid neglecting research. Ensure you gain an accurate understanding of their perspectives and realities.

Chapter 26

Preventing flat and inconsistent characters

Creating flat and inconsistent characters can seriously undermine the quality of your story. Avoid common pitfalls such as abrupt character changes, stereotypes, and heavy exposition. When you master the art of crafting complex and consistent characters, your story greatly benefits. We'll explore strategies to prevent the creation of flat and inconsistent characters and instead develop memorable and coherent ones.

1. Psychological depth

Psychological depth is key to avoiding flat characters. Dive into the psychology of your characters by exploring their motivations, hidden desires, fears, and internal conflicts.

2. Goals and obstacles

Each character should have clear goals and obstacles to overcome. These elements give characters a purpose in the story and create opportunities for the development of their psychology.

3. Psychological consistency

Consistency is essential to avoid inconsistent characters. Ensure that the actions, words, and thoughts of your characters align with their established psychology.

4. Well-defined character arcs

Define the character arcs of your characters from the beginning of the story. Well-planned character arcs help prevent sudden and unmotivated changes in character.

5. Internal and external motivations

Characters should be motivated by both internal and external factors. Explore their deep motivations, such as personal desires, past traumas, and moral dilemmas.

6. Meaningful relationships

Interactions between characters are essential for the development of their psychology. Create meaningful relationships that influence how characters evolve.

7. Gradual evolution

Characters should evolve gradually throughout the story. Avoid abrupt character changes by building their development gradually.

8. Research and authenticity

If you're writing about characters with cultural backgrounds, professions, or experiences different from your own, conduct thorough research to ensure the authenticity of their psychology.

9.External feedback

Have your work read by beta readers or reviewers to get external feedback on your characters' psychology. External perspectives can reveal inconsistencies or gaps you might not have noticed.

10. Continuous revision

Regularly revisit the psychology of your characters during the writing process. Ensure that their development remains consistent, and their psychology is well-developed.

Part 10

Case studies and analyses

Chapter 27

Analysis of famous literary characters

To understand how to create memorable characters, it is valuable to analyze examples of famous literary characters. We will examine some of these characters and explore what makes them so remarkable from a psychological perspective.

1. Jay Gatsby - "The Great Gatsby" by F. Scott Fitzgerald

Jay Gatsby is a complex character who hides deep desires and past traumas behind his facade of a wealthy and mysterious man. His obsession with Daisy Buchanan drives his character, and his troubled past is gradually revealed, creating intriguing psychology.

2. Holden Caulfield - "The Catcher in the Rye" by J.D. Salinger

Holden Caulfield is a teenager struggling against a world he perceives as hypocritical. His inner thoughts, doubts, and rebellions against the superficiality of society make him an iconic character in young adult literature.

3. Elizabeth Bennet - "Pride and Prejudice" by Jane Austen

Elizabeth Bennet is a heroine with a strong personality and sharp intelligence. Her independent character and ability to challenge social conventions make her a pioneering female character in 19th-century literature.

4. Sherlock Holmes - Works by Sir Arthur Conan Doyle

Sherlock Holmes is a legendary detective whose psychology revolves around his brilliant intellect and his dependence on cocaine. His ability to analyze the smallest details and solve complex mysteries makes him a fascinating character.

5. Hamlet - "Hamlet" by William Shakespeare

Hamlet is a character tormented by existential doubts, moral dilemmas, and internal conflicts. His complex psychology is highlighted in his introspective soliloquies, making him one of the most studied characters in dramatic literature.

6. Scarlett O'Hara - "Gone with the Wind" by Margaret Mitchell

Scarlett O'Hara is a multifaceted heroine, transitioning from frivolity to resilience throughout the story. Her psychology is shaped by the upheavals of the American Civil War and her quest for survival.

7. Severus Snape - The "Harry Potter" series by J.K. Rowling

Severus Snape is an ambiguous character with complex psychology. His deep motivations, shifting alliances, and well-guarded secrets make him an intriguing character whose true nature is gradually revealed.

8. Bilbo Baggins - "The Hobbit" by J.R.R. Tolkien

Bilbo Baggins is a character who evolves from discomfort and fear to adventure and bravery. His psychology is shaped by his desire for comfort, but he ultimately discovers a deep inner resilience.

9. Atticus Finch - "To Kill a Mockingbird" by Harper Lee

Atticus Finch is a moral and benevolent character whose psychology is evident in his commitment to justice and his efforts to educate his children about life's fundamental values.

10. Hester Prynne - "The Scarlet Letter" by Nathaniel Hawthorne

Hester Prynne is a heroine marked by public shame and solitude. Her psychology revolves around her quest

for redemption and her determination to protect her
illegitimate child.

Chapter 28

How writers use character psychology

Character psychology is a powerful tool in the writer's arsenal when aiming to create narratives rich in emotion, meaning, and memorability. It allows for the exploration of universal themes, the establishment of emotional connections with readers, and the bringing to life of unforgettable characters. Writers use psychology to add depth to their stories and to examine the human condition from various perspectives. We will explore how writers use character psychology to craft engaging narratives and convey profound themes and messages.

1. The development of the narrative plot

Character psychology is often the driving force behind the narrative plot. The desires, motivations, and internal conflicts of characters create situations, obstacles, and stakes that propel the story forward.

2. Exploration of universal themes

Characters often serve as vehicles to explore universal themes such as love, loss, redemption, morality, and identity. Their experiences and psychology allow writers to examine these themes from different perspectives.

3. Building an emotional connection with readers

Well-developed and psychologically rich characters enable readers to identify, become attached to, and feel empathy toward them. This emotional connection makes the story more immersive and impactful.

4. Exploring the human condition

Character psychology allows for an exploration of the complexity of the human condition. Characters can reflect the struggles, hopes, and challenges faced by humans in reality.

5. Creating memorable characters

Psychologically rich and nuanced characters remain etched in the memory of readers long after closing the book. Writers use psychology to craft memorable and unforgettable characters.

6. The evolution of characters

Character psychology is essential in showcasing how characters evolve throughout the story. Well-developed character arcs allow for a compelling depiction of characters' transformations.

7. Creating tension and conflict

The internal conflicts and moral dilemmas of characters add tension to the story. Writers use psychology to create situations where characters are faced with challenging choices.

8. Revealing human complexities

Character psychology reveals the intricacies of human nature. Characters are neither entirely good nor entirely bad but rather a mosaic of qualities and flaws.

9. Creating convincing antagonists

Well-developed antagonists have a psychology that explains their actions and perspective. Writers use psychology to add depth to antagonists and make their motivations understandable.

10. Using psychology in the fictional world

Character psychology also influences how the fictional world is constructed. Settings, social rules, and events are shaped by the psychology of the characters.

Chapter 29

Final tips on mastering character psychology

Character psychology is a fundamental element of literary creation. It brings memorable characters to life, explores universal themes, and creates emotional connections with readers. By mastering the concepts and techniques presented in this book, you are well-equipped to create unforgettable heroes and antagonists. This final chapter aims to guide you on the path of continuous improvement in your writing skills.

1. Practice, practice, practice

Mastering character psychology, like any skill, requires practice. Write regularly and create new characters to refine your skills.

2. Read abundantly

Reading is an invaluable source of inspiration and learning. Read a variety of genres and authors to study how different writers use character psychology.

3. Study human psychology

A deep understanding of human psychology is essential for creating authentic characters. Read books on psychology, explore human behaviors and motivations, and stay informed about advancements in the field.

4. Solicit feedback and revisions

Share your work with other writers, critique groups, or beta readers to receive constructive feedback on the psychology of your characters. Be prepared to revise and enhance your work accordingly.

5. Explore new horizons

Don't be afraid to explore new horizons in character psychology. Create characters that defy stereotypes and are unique to your writing style.

6. Listen to your characters

Sometimes, your characters will come to life on their own and guide you in their development. Listen to their inner voice and be open to organic changes in their psychology.

7. Seek depth

Always strive to add depth to your characters. Dig deeper into their psychology, motivations, and emotions to create a richer reading experience.

8.Be patient and persevere

Mastering character psychology is a journey that takes time. Be patient with yourself and persevere in your quest for improvement.

9. Keep learning

Writing is a constantly evolving field. Keep learning, exploring new techniques, and staying informed about literary trends to remain a competent writer.

10. Share Your Passion

Share your passion for character psychology with other writers. Participate in writing workshops, online discussion groups, or literary events to enrich your understanding and network.

By continuing to practice, study, explore, and persevere, you can create characters that captivate readers, evoke emotions, and bring your stories to life.

www.ingramcontent.com/pod-product-compliance
Lightning Source LLC
Chambersburg PA
CBHW031304250726
48656CB00005B/1633